UKULELE MUSIC

D0587572

PETER READING

Book I   *Ukulele Music*
Book II   *Going On*

SECKER & WARBURG
LONDON

First published in England 1985 by
Martin Secker & Warburg Limited
54 Poland Street, London W1V 3DF

Copyright © Peter Reading 1985

British Library Cataloguing in Publication Data

Reading, Peter
Ukulele music.
I. Title
821'.914   PR 6068.E27

ISBN 0–346–40986–0

Typeset by Inforum Ltd, Portsmouth
Printed in England by
Redwood Burn Ltd, Trowbridge

ACKNOWLEDGEMENTS

Some of the material has appeared in *Encounter*, the Poetry Book Society *Supplement* (1985), *Poetry Review*, *Thames Poetry* and *The Times Literary Supplement*, or been broadcast on BBC Radio 3.

Book I is dedicated to John Christopher; Book II to Mark Pitter.

BOOK I

UKULELE MUSIC

Dear sir,

I come in this morning instead of tomorrow as I have to take ~~Budige~~ ~~bugdie~~ Bird to the Vets, as he got out of cage door for the first time, By <u>accident.</u> As I was putting seed in. & taking out sand sheet. He went mad. & banged himself against THE wall. & fell down on to the Magic coal fire. got jammed in the back of coal effect. Broken leg and side of his body awfull state. he is in. good job fire was not on.

faithly Viv

p.S. could you oblige the next weeks money this wk. be in tomorrow Morning, Only the Capting which I chars for tuesdays has let me off this Tues but has PAID yrs Viv

3

Few atrocities
of which H. sap. *can conceive*
remain unfulfilled

'They must have been about 17/18, possibly 19:
one, tattooed on his hand MAM; one, tattooed on his arm LOVE.

One of them grabbed at my handbag but I just belted him with it,
caught him one under the ear, then I yelled "Somebody, help!"

Even although it was lunchtime and several people were
watching
nobody wanted to know. Two women just walked right past.'

She had been pushing her 8-month-old, Sharen-Jayne, in the
buggy.
Now the kid started to scrawk; one of our heroes smirked, spat,

fondled the empty pint bottle he had in his hand and then
smashed it
on an adjacent brick wall, held the bits to the child's throat.

'I said "Hurt me if you like but don't injure the innocent baby –
it can't defend itself, see? Don't do it don't do it *please!*"

He said "If I do the baby I'll get what I want, so I'll cut it."
He shoved the glass in her cheek; twisted the jagged edge in.

He told me "This is how we earn our living, this and the dole
like."
Then he just wiggled the sharp, smashed slivers into her eye.'

Promptly the mother gave over her golden wedding-ring, also
three pounds in cash and a watch (silver, engraved 'My True
Love'),

but the attackers slashed Sharen twice more – in the mouth, and a
deep cut
neatly round one chubby knee. Then they strolled leisurely off.

4

'Sharen was screaming and bleeding a lot and I thought they had killed her.'

C.I.D. officers say 'This is a callous assault . . .'

Dear Sir,

will finish of your hoovering and such tomorrow as my hand is still bad, my right one. As last wk. there is a lady two doors off me has a bitch and a little boy over the road had been playing with it. and since then where all the dogs come from I do not know. But one of them had pinned the boy against the wall. I ran out with a hand full of pepper to throw at the dogs face. I throw it. but it had bit me in the hand. just above my right thumb where the bone is. I ran after the dog. with a whitening brush also and I fell also over the fence. bruised my knee's. But my knee is alright. My hand I have sufferd. The dog got put down to sleep. I have been to Hospitle But I heard later. that another dog had pinned the same boy he is only four yrs old. and MARLD him in the face and eyes he has had 5 stitches across his left eye. The other dog also had to be put down to sleep I tell you it has been awfull over there with the dogs. The woman who the bitch belongs to, had forgotten she had left her kitchen window open One of the dogs had jump in through the window. her Husband had delt with the dog. But slammed the kitchen window and all of the glass had fallen out in pieces. (It is awfull. when the little girls are about.) There mothers have to keep them in. or take them with them. the pain is going all the way up my arm. I have had a TECNAS. you know, a little RED CARD.

YRS Viv.

6

Someone has left a whole crateful of empty lemonade bottles
on the pedestrian bridge. Here come three ten-year-old boys.

Queuing for buses, the off-peak shoppers are gathered together
under the cast concrete span (aerosolled WANKERS and TREV).

Each of the children has picked up an empty and, quite nonchal-
antly,
hurls it down onto the grans, young mums and spinsters and
babes.

No one evinces surprise or alarm or even vexation,
fox-trotting through the smashed bits, Terpsichorean and deft.

Each boy throws four bottles, spits from the parapet into our
faces,
shouts 'Fucking bastards' and yelps. Glass crunches under a bus.

Blood smears the calf of an elderly lady silently weeping.
'Kids' our conductor observes 'should be done something about.'

Grans are bewildered by post-Coronation disintegration; offspring of offspring of *their* offspring infest and despoil.

('You think you're doing a fine job of work don't you, oh yes, but you're not. Stop it stop it, it's dirty dirty dirty in the streets like that' an old woman shopper informs two boys of ten or eleven who slouch against a butcher's window in busy Northcote Rd., SW11. Moist beige tripes gleam. Around the Chopper bikes blobs of bubbly saliva streaked green and yellow describe a semi-circle on the greasy pavement. The boys giggle and one of them remarks sotto voce 'Fuck off old cow'. 'What did you say?' They giggle and do not answer. One boy spits afresh at his colleague's cycle. A glycerite sac depends from the canary-coloured spokes, elongates gradually. 'Dirty little devils. Look at them look at them!' she appeals to those of us nearby. We evince neither surprise nor concern. She turns begrudgingly. Silver streaks jet concurrently from gaps between the front teeth of each boy. She continues upon her way unaware that her pink leatherette mac is sullied by twin viscid drools.)

Stubbornly, Taffs, at their damn-fool anachronistic eisteddfods,
still, with this breach in the hull, twang (ineffectual lyres).

Mercury falls, it's no go, and the pink geraniums shrivel:
ceilidh and Old Viennese drone as the packet goes down.

When all the cities were felled by the pongoid subspecies in them
(Belfast, Jerusalem, Brum., Liverpool, Beirut) and when

blood-swilling (Allah is wonderful) Middle-East Yahoos had
purchased
nuclear hardware, he found distich the only form apt.

Too Many Of Us and Dwindled Resources and War had undone
us.
Matter impartially throve (quark, strangeness, charm) not as *us*.

Sing in Your Bath if You Want to Seem Sexy and **Blood-Bath in
Jordan**
vie for front page in the tabs. Doh ray me fah soh lah te

well, Sir

Only, the Capting has said I was not really wanted so I have gone to you instead. only. You are not here as you know. So have let myself in with spare key but he has PAY me just the same as he is kind old man with heart of gold etc. and has told me how underneath. and he has seen it with OWN eyes so knows it is true. where I thought it was just Underground Car Park ect. under ~~Civic~~ Civet Centre is not just Car Park but bunk for FALL if there is trouble, that sometimes seems likely with uSA and russiens with there bomb warfair. But what can you do? nothing and he say there are SARDINES stored in there for after siren. with DRINK. so we are all prepared thank God. But what I want to know is when you vote the different Goverments do NOT do what you ask do they? Because I want NO TROUBLE but it seems no difference what you want the Rulers just do a DIFFERENT THING. So you can only keep CHEERFUL and keep trying your best. sir. for Exsample I have done the floors but their is one of Yr writings there that ALAS is swept in the Hoover bag, and I got it out all right but is VERY twisted with the thing that BEATS as SWEEPS as CLEANS the one about a Piano and a Man AND woman that I think is DIRTY but it takes all sorts and did you REALLY work at such a club in uSA? I never knew you had been there but I would not want sardines ALL THE TIME who would? noone. but it would be <u>emergency</u> like in the last one where it was tin sheeting. But now they are on the streets the ARMY against thugs and Mugers as that is where the REAL war is on NOW, cities in 2 halfs with police and army and nice folks against dirty animals, so may HAVE to go DOWN soon for THAT war. But I have throw it away, the poetry writing on the Piano at top of kitchin bin VERY TOP if you want it back.

and Oblige Viv.

Beetrooty colonels explain to the Lounge Bar how, in the 'Last
                                                              Show',
they had a marvellous time, and how we need a new war

if we are going to get this Great Country back on its feet, sir
(also all beards should be shaved: also the Dole should be
                                                        stopped).

Life still goes on and *It isn't the end of the world* (the child-soothing
platitudes weaken now Cruise proves them potentially false).

Lieder's no art against these sorry times (anguished Paramour
                                                          likens
mountainy crags and a crow to the flint heart of his Frau).

Dear sir,

have done some hoover of the front room. but am going now be back tomorrow morning if you can oblige with next week money same as last time. Only my sister. not the one in Australia the other one here. was standing at the bus station when boys threw bottles and ones broken glass flew up and cut leg BAD CUT. only about ten also, she says so must go and help as she is lost a husband recently too. I tell you no one knows how bad it is here with these children ALL OVER. They will be the death of us no mistake. also the world situtation no better, America Russia jews and Arabians irish and such. what can you do as it gets worse like one of yr poetry Works that I saw when cleaning desk with wax which I need more of soon as possible please. The same as in the empty tin. but well what can you do only get on with it. as you cant' sort it all out can you? we are like the man in music Hall song that goes he play his Uku uker Youkalaylee while the ship went down. *only we all have problems like my sister and Goverments so can only carry on best we can, the next weeks money this week please as am short due to various things and the new wax pollish Viv.*

PS. doctor said it is not SO bad but has had 6 stitch.

Glossy black slices of smooth slab are all laid facing towards due
East – in the twerpish conceit sunrise might pleasure them *now*!

Glittery gilt lists the names and the dates and the bullshit about
them
– 'Fell Asleep', 'Gone to Rest' (tcha!), 'Resting in Jesus' Arms'
(pah!).

'Gone Where We'll All Join Again on the Happy Shore Everafter'
(spew, vomit, puke, throw-up, retch), 'Went Without Saying
Goodbye'.

Inside a shed with the Council's coat-of-arms blazoned on it
there is a Flymo and spades. Here comes a gent with a pick:

'Wouldn't it make you want to dip your bread in the piss-pot
– some of the bilge they write there? Fuckin daft sods' (he opines).

Sweet peas are cunningly wrought in a huge pink crucifix resting
fresh on damp just-replaced turf. Wet clay outlines a new slot.

Biro-smudged sympathy-cards blow about and one is signed
'Viv, The
Depest Regrett Always Felt' (it shows a wren on a wreath).

On a diminutive gravy-hued sandstone wafer is chiselled
that which, despite mawkishness, prompts a sharp intake of
breath.

Aged 10.
Little Boy,
We Would Not
Wake You To
Suffer Again.

Oh sir,

only I havnt known. which way to TURN since the Funeral. It was the sisters youngest such a good lad too and only ten it seems wrong. somehow, and they would play in the streets though they was told often enough GOD only knows. So it was a bus when they was playing football and the poor little mite had gone when they got him. to the Hospitle so that is why I didnt' come for 3 days but was in this morning and hope you find this note behind the tea pot and with thanks for the new Polish which have done the desk and chairs with. My oldest Trevor has been TOWER OF strenth since tragdy but <u>will</u> get those tatoos just like his DAD in that way just last week got MAM done on his hand which is nice he is a good lad to his Mother and a Tower. So can I have last weeks moneys though I did not come and not have money next week instead. Only the flowers which was a cross of pink flowers. very nicely done. do cost such a lot not that you bigrudge it do you when its your own Sisters youngest? So if you could leave it buy the dusters and furnature wax it will be fine tomorrow.

Obliged, Viv.

PS we take her to the zoo next weekend to take her out of herself. the sister. as it will be a nice change our Trevor says.

14

'Them animals is disgusting.'

In London Zoo is a large flat painted Disneyesque lion
sporting a circular hole cut where the face ought to be.

On its reverse is a step upon which the visitor stands and
puts his own face through the hole – so that he may be thus
snapped.

So, the resultant photograph shows the face of a friend or
relative grinning like mad out of a leonine frame.

This seems to be a very popular piece of equipment –
Arabs in nightshirts and Japs queue with Jews. Polaroids click.

Tabloids blown underfoot headline a couple of global débâcles.
Gran, from the lion's mouth, leers: toothless, cadaverous, blithe.

Oh it is very funny to put your head through the facial
orifice of a joke lion – races and creeds are agreed.

Down the old Monkey House there is a *Cercopithecus* wanking
and a baboon (with its thumb stuck up its arse) to revile.

Dear Sir didnt come in yesterday as planned as I lost key and how it happened was this. that we went to zoo with sister and the children which was the sister lost her youngest. And while we was throwing a ten pence for luck onto back of Allergator corcodile which is in Tropical House it must have fell from my purse. Everyone throws money for luck onto back of this Reptille and his pool is FULL of two P ten P and 5P pieces which bring GOOD LUCK to thrower. So had to go yesterday to see if the keeper had found it. he had and said they empty pool every month and spend money. It buys keepers there beer he says they get POUNDS so I got key back that is why I am here today instead but unfortunatly have by ACCIDENT spoilt one of your papers with poetry on it that was on yr desk as I threw it on the Parkray by mistake. and hope this is no inconvenience or can you do another one instead? Sister much better since outing but oldest boy Trev in trouble with police who came last night to house but I dont believe it as he is a good boy. But she is perking up a bit now and was cheerful at weekend and my boy took a Poloid Photo of her with head through a LION which was V. funny and makes her laugh which is good for her. Police say he has mugged but it canot be as he is GOOD BOY.

faithly VIV. p.s. worse things happen at SEA!

'Life is too black as he paints it' and 'Reading's nastiness some-
times
seems a bit over the top' thinks a review – so does *he*.

Too black and over the top, though, is what the Actual often
happens to be, I'm afraid. He don't *invent* it, you know.

Take, for example, some snippets from last week's dailies before
they're
screwed up to light the Parkray: Birmingham, March '83,

on her allotment in King's Heath, picking daffodils, Dr
Dorris McCutcheon (retired) pauses to look at her veg.

Dr McCutcheon (aged 81) does not know that behind her,
Dennis (aged 36) lurks, clutching an old iron bar.

Unemployed labourer Dennis Bowering sneaks up behind her,
bashes her over the head – jaw, nose and cheek are smashed-in.

Dennis then drags her until he has got her into the tool-shed,
strikes her again and again, there is a sexual assault,

also a watch and some money worth less than ten pounds are
stolen.
'Is an appalling offence . . .' Bowering is told by the Judge.

Amateur frogmen discover a pair of human legs buried
Mafia-style in cement, deep in an Austrian lake.

Smugly, Americans rail over KA 007;
angrily, Moscow retorts. Hokkaido fishermen find

five human bits of meat, one faceless limbless female Caucasian,
shirts, empty briefcases, shoes, fragments of little child's coat,

pieces of movable section of wing of a 747,
one piece of human back flesh (in salmon-fishermen's nets),

one headless human too mangled to ascertain what the sex is.
USA/USSR butcher a Boeing like chess

(probably civil jumbos *are* used for Intelligence business;
pity the poor sods on board don't have the chance to opt out).

Sexual outrage on woman of 88 robbed of her savings.
Finger found stuck on barbed wire. Too black and over the top.

Clearly we no longer hold *H. sapiens* in great reverence
(which situation, alas, no elegiacs can fix).

What do they think they're playing at, then, these Poetry Wal-
lahs?
Grub St. reviewing its own lame valedictory bunk.

dear Sir,

well I have hooverd and wax pollish the desk so I will collect money tomorrow. There is trouble on our block since my Tom plays the bones to tunes of George Formby and was due to give a TURN at the club tonight but was paralitic last night and WOULD try to practise and of course one of them. the bones. went over next door and the woman there that has the bitch that MARLD the child well her bitch grabs the bone but my Tom shouts abuse and. of course the outcome is there is a window broke. Which the man next door have only just mended after the last trouble. so we will see how it goes tonight at the Club he does that one he played his Youkerlaylie as the Ship Went down. and I know how He felt, because it is the same with my eldest Trevor who is REPRIMANDED IN CUS-TARDY as the policeman put it who is a nice man but I know my lad is innerscent of that awful thing they say he done. But these things are sent to TRY Us as my Man says and I hope he plays his bones well tonight. just like he did that year we were in the T.V. show Mr and Mrs, did you know we were in it? yes in Llandudno and he entertained the crowds they were in stitches when the ONE MAN BAND never turned up. so I have used up all the Johnsons Wax again so please oblige, We all have problems even the different Parlerments, also the police Forces. as well as me, and you with Yr writings

Viv, P.S. we can only carry on the best we can manage

Down at the PDSA there's a queue of unprepossessing
buggered-up budgies and dogs. Someone is telling how Rex

quite unaccountably ('Never been known to act like it previous')
set on the nipper next door, and must now 'get put to sleep'.

'Even although he has done such a thing – and that to a kiddy –
I can't help loving him still – you *have* to stand by your own.'

'That's what I feels about my eldest (Trev) – they've done him for
mugging –
still, you *must* still love your own; if he's bad, he's *still* my boy.'

Cotton wool tenderly placed in a shoe-box comforts a frail life.
There is much love at the Vet's – even for bad dogs and Trev.

Was one time anchored in forty
fathom near unto the shore
of Mascarenhas Island.
Landed, we found blue pigeons
so tame as to suffer us
to capture them by our hands
so that we killed and roasted
above two hundred the first day.
Also we took many others –
grey paraquets, wild geese
and penguins (which last hath but stumps
for wings, so cannot fly).
Most entertaining to catch
a paraquet and make it
cry aloud till the rest
of its kind flocked round it and thus
enabled themselves to be caught.
Twenty five turtle, lying
under one tree, was taken.

On then to St. Mary's Island,
where we careened, and thence
stood for the Straights of Sunda.

At 5° 30'
south of the line, the alarm
'Fire!' was raised – the steward
had gone below for brandy,
thrust candle into the hole
of a cask on the tier above
whence he drew his spirits, and when
removing his candle, a spark
had fell from the wick down the bung,
igniting the spirit. He poured

water unto the cask,
by which we had thought to choke it.

But the flames, reviving, blew out
the cask ends, when the fire
reached to a heap of coals
stowed there, which, lighted, gave off
a thick sulphureous smoke
thwarting attempts to extinguish it.

In this emergency
I appealed to the supercargo
to cast overboard all powder.
But (stubborn, arrogant, greedy,
as so many of his class)
he refused. Says he 'To throw
our powder away is to risk
attack from our enemies'.

Meantime the rage of the fire
augmented more and more.
We scuttled decks that greater
floods of water could be
got into ye hold, but all
attempts proved vain.

                    I resolved
to summon the carpenters
with augers to bore the hull
that water might enter below
and quench the flames.

                    But our oil
ignited then, d'ye see?,
and with sixty five good men
I stood on deck by the main
hatchway receiving buckets
when the powder, 300 kegs,
was reached.

            The vessel blew up
into the air with one hundred
and nineteen souls: a moment
afterwards, not one single
human being was seen:
believing myself to be launched
into eternity,
I cried out aloud for Mercy.

Some slender remnant of life
and resolution still lurked
in my heart. I gained the wreck,
as was gone to a thousand pieces,
clung to a yard.

            The long-boat,
got off afore the explosion
by a deserting faction,
now, in the very worst
of my extremity,
ran to the place with all speed,
whereat the trumpeter
threw out a line by which
I obtained that frail haven
of temporary ease,
and hymned being simply extant.

Cast up, one time, wrecked,
on bleak Patagonia
out of the Wager, Indiaman,
Commodore Anson's squadron.
Six years, afore we reached home.

Only food, shellfish and raw seal –
as we managed to stone unto death
or found dead, raw, rank, rotted.

Reduced thus to misery,
and so emaciated,
we scarce resembled mankind.
At nights in hail and snow
with naught but open beach
to lay down upon in order
to procure a little rest –
oftentimes having to pull off
the few rags I was left wearing,
it being impossible
to sleep with them on for the vermin
as by that time swarmed about them;
albeit, I often removed
my sark and, laying it down
on a boulder, beat it hard
with an huge stone, hoping to slay
an hundred of them at once,
for it were endless work
to pick them off one by one.
What we suffered from this
was worse even than the hunger.
But we were cleanly compared
of our captain, for I could compare
his body to nothing more like

an ant hill, so many thousand
of vermin crawling over it;
for he were past attempting
to rid himself in the least
of this torment, as he had quite
lost himself, not recollecting
our names that were about him,
nor his own. His beard as long
as an hermit's: that and his face
being besmirched of filth
from having been long accustomed
himself to sleep on a bag
in which he kept stinking seal meat
(which prudent measure he took
to prevent our getting at it
as he slept). His legs swelled huge
as mill-posts, whilst his torso
was as a skin packet of bones –
and upon bleached seal bones he played
hour after hour in uncanny
tattoo as to harmonize
with a wordless mindless dirge
as he moithered, moithered, moithered,
weird, xysterical airs,
yea, even unto the end.

Was one time cast on Oroolong,
when the Antelope packet went down.
The king of Coorooraa
succoured us, gave us meat,
in return of which we shewed him
the swivel as we had salvaged
out of the wreck, and the six-
pounder and our small-arms.
He and his natives were thrilled
and astonished. A flying squirrel
having settled upon a tree
nearby, our captain's servant
loaded his musquet, shot it.
Seeing the animal drop
off of a lofty tree's top,
without, apparently,
anything passing to it,
they ran to take it up;
when, perceiving the holes,
they chuckled, evidenced glee
and begged to be allowed
guns for themselves that they might
do slaughter of their near neighbours
whom they were desirous to see
fall, full of holes, as this,
dead in great quantity.
We acquiesced.

                    They made
great execution with these,
our fire-arms, puzzling their foes,
who could not comprehend
how that their people dropped
without receiving any
apparent blow. Though holes
were seen in their bodies, they couldn't
divine by what agency

they were thus, in a moment, deprived
of motion and life. The whole
of the prisoners taken was shot.
We objected upon this last,
explained inhumanity
unto ye simple minds.

Their king gave unto us then
a kind of victory banquet,
whereat one tar of our number,
who out of the wreck had saved
an Italian violin
and had the bowing of it,
struck up. I know not whether
twas due to the victory,
or the feast, or to the grog
of which we allowed them a plenty,
or whether the fiddle musick;
but, be it whichever, they reeled,
cavorted like monkeys and fell
euphoric with our company
unto ye general dust.

Sailed one time aboard
trawler the Lucky Dragon,
crew o' 23,
hundred miles off Bikini,
in the March of '54.

Tars was all below
down in the a'ter-cabin;
crew man, Suzuki,
run abaft a-hollering
'The sun rises in the West!'

Hands mustered on deck,
saw, to larboard, a fireball,
like a rainbow brand,
rise up from ye horizon,
silent, that was the queer thing.

Minutes passed; the blast
suddenly shook the ocean,
shuddered our whole hulk,
hands was belayed with affright,
none, howsomdever, hurt (*then*).

But the skies turned *strange* –
misty wi' weird white ashes
as *swirled*, d'ye see?,
down onto decks, men, rigging . . .
That ash made us ill (*later*).

Most awful, terrific form
shipwreck can take is fire;
where the unfortunate
victims has only two
alternatives – to seek death
in one element in order
to avoid it in another.

One time the enemy's powder
(with whom we was close-engaged)
took fire – match left a-purpose
by their skipper, damn his eyes –
both the vessels blew up,
most violent dreadful explosion.

We, the spectators, ourselves
were the poor players also
in the bloody scene – some thinking
maybe it were the Last Judgement,
confounded, unable to gauge
whether or no we beheld it –
two ships hurled up on high
two hundred fathoms in air,
where there was formed a mountain
of fire, water and wreck;
dread conflagration below,
cannon unpeeling above,
rending of masts and planks,
ripping of canvas and cordage,
screams, like stuck pigs, of brent tars.

When the ship first took fire
I was blowed clean from the forecastle,
fell back into the sea
where I remained under water
unable to gain ye surface,
struggled as one afeared

of drowning, got up and seized
a bulk of mast as I found
nearby.

        Saw floating about
divers wounded and dead –
two half bodies, with still
some remnant of life, a-rising
and sinking, rising and sinking,
leaving the deep dyed pink.
Deplorable to behold
scores of limbs and fragments
of bodies – most of them spitted
on splintered timbers and spars.

Survivors we boarded a boat
almost entire from the wreck.
Most of us vomited constant
from swallowing pints of sea water.

I suffered long and swelled
to a surprising degree,
all my hair, face and one side
of my body were brent with powder;
bled at the mouth, nose, ears
(I know not whether this
be the effect of powder,
by swelling up the vessels
containing the blood of our bodies
to such extent that the ends
of the veins open and ooze it;
or whether it be occasioned
by the great noise and violent
motion in the same organs –
but let it happen which way
it will, there was no room there then
for consulting of physicians).

31

Thro the long night some sang,
attempting to keep up spirits.
Merciful Providence
preserving some measure of wine
and rum from the hold, the mate
contrived then to engineer
a musical instrument
on which he made bold to play.

Since I have so often felt
the malignant influence
of the stars presiding over
the seas, and by adverse fortune
lost all the wealth which, with such
trouble and care, I amassed,
it has been no source of pleasure
recalling to memory
the disasters that have assailed us.

Still, as a singer a song
or an old player an air,
I am impelled to convey
salt observations, a tar's
chantey habit, d'ye see?

I know not whether we've bid
adieu to the sea, or whether
we shall set forth again
where we have known such mischief;
whether traverse the ocean
in quest of a little wealth;
or rest in quiet and consume
what our relations have left us.

Our strange propensity
to undertake voyages,
alike to that of gaming –
whatever adversity
befalls us, we trust, at length,
prosperity shall o'ertake us,
therefore continue to play.

So with us at sea,
for, whatever calamity
we meet with, we hope for some
chance opportunity
to indemnify our losses.

And shall it, now, be counted
as ye dignified defiance
in us towards our fateful
merciless element,
or gull naiveté,
cousin to recklessness,
that, e'en in pitching Gulphward,
our salt kind brings forth chanteys?

Who would have thought it Sir, actually putting ME in a WRITING!
me and the Capting and ALL. What a turn up for the books.

Only, I must say I do not know HOW them people in poems
manage to say what they want – you know, in funny short lines,

or like what YOU do with them ones of yours sir, made of two lines like.
Still, when you're USED to it like, then you can speak natural.

Only, the newspaper man said that you was TRYING to sound like
low classes voices and that, only you wasn't no good –

you know, the CUTTING you left on yr desk top when I was waxing –
you know, that CRICKET which said you wasn't no good at all?

when you got TERRIBLE, stamping and raging calling him stupid
and how the man was a FOOL, which was the day you took DRINK.

'What is to one class of minds and perceptions exaggeration,
is to another plain truth' (Dickens remarks in a brief

preface to *Chuzzlewit*). 'I have not touched one character straight
                                                              from
life, but some counterpart of that very character has

asked me, incredulous, "Really now *did you* ever see, *really*,
anyone *really* like that?" ' (this is the gist, not precise).

Well I can tell that old cricket that this is JUST how we speaks like,
me and the Capting and all (only not just in two lines).

One time, returning to home port, fell in with Englishman (16-gunner) bound England from Spain; hailed her heave-to and
                                                            belay.

After a skirmish we forced her to strike her colours and seized
                                                              her.
Auctioned her off at Rochelle; carried the prize to Bordeaux.

Our tars had been so long absent from home that now we
                                                    indulged in
every extravagant vice, ere we be called to ye Deep.

Merchants advanced us, without hesitation, money and goods
                                                              on
promise of that which was our share of the booty, d'ye see?

We spent the night in whatever amusements best pleased our
                                                           fancy –
claret and gore and the stench of ye rank pox-festered trulls.

We spent the next day traversing the town in masquerade,
                                                          ranting,
had ourselves carried in chairs, lighted with torches, at noon.

As we caroused thus abroad we caused music, plucked forth
                                                    from gambas
boldly, t'embellish the raw, rude Dionysian debauch.

And the drear consequence of this gross wanton mass indiscre-
                                                            tion
was the untimely demise of damned near all the whole crew.

Jimmy 'The Beard' Ferrozzo, aged 40, Manager of the
Condor Club, where I now work (down San Francisco's North
                                                           Beach),

died when the stage-prop piano we use for Carol the stripper
pinned him tight into the roof, causing his breathing to stop.

Mr Boyd Stephens, the medical guy who did the autopsy,
said that Ferrozzo was pressed so tight he couldn't inhale,

said that 'Compression Asphyxia' is the name of the ball-game –
pressure had squashed up the chest so hard it couldn't expand.

I have been Caretaker down at the topless Condor Club now for,
must be a couple of years. When I unlocked, 9 a.m.,

I found Ferrozzo draped over his girlfriend (23-year-old
Trixie – this slag from the Club, nude Go-Go dancer, you know?).

She had no clothes on and she was stuck, screaming, under him –
it was
three hours before she could be freed by the cops from the raised

Steinway, a prop they have used at the Club for 2 decades almost
(topless star Carol descends, sprawled on the keys, to the stage).

Even now, no one knows what caused the joke piano to rise up
into the ceiling, 12 ft., pinning Ferrozzo and Trix.

Police say the motor that operates on the lifting device had
burned out and couldn't be switched so as to bring it back down.

Some way the Manager's body had kept her 2 or 3 inches
off of the ceiling and stopped Trixie herself being crushed.

Det. Whitney Gunther says: 'She was so drunk she doesn't
remember
laying down nude on the strings inside the grand – she just
knows

sometime that a.m. she woke up to hear the twanging of taut
wires.'
Man! What an Exit, you know? Welter of plucked gut and spunk.

*Only, because it has broke (I.T.V.) we HAD to watch 'Seasars' –
stories about the roam Kings, dirty disgusting old lot.*

*One of them dressed up in smelly old skins and rushed out at captives
wounding there PRIVATES with KNIFE. also had LOVED his own
Mam.*

*this is called 'Narrow' which plays on a fiddle, all the time Roam burnd
but why it Brakes is because. my man has FIXED it last week*

*Also my mack is at cleaners because of kiddies which MARK it
ever so bad with their spit. They should be children of Roam –*

*what with the way they go on with their dirty, horrible, habbits
One of which made them all HEAR while he plays music all nite.*

*This one is known as 'Callegulum' which is v. funny name for
King but is THERE on t.v. So must be right. it is pink*

*leather effect with a belt and the reason why there is broken
glass on Barometer is: cutting a LONG story short.*

*My man is playing it just as a banjo, being the SAME SHAPE,
singing the George Formby Song. and he has drop it on FLOOR*

*SO that the glass and the silvery stuff you get in it all come
out and can not be got back. One of them SAWED men in half*

also he has a poor soul stabbed to death with terrible pen nibs
also a mans' brains flogged out using a CHAIN for three days

which is the same sort of thing that you get in newspaper these days.
what with the Irish and that. so I have bought a new GAMP.

That is because of the Mack but he also made FATHER's go to
SEE their own kiddies killed dead, that was the worst thing of all

so it has broke and the needle now ALWAYS points to the STORMY –
he is a fool to have PLAYED (Formby) But ROAM is BAD TIME

Nero springs out girt in lynx pelts and slits slave's dick with a
                                                        razor . . .
ROAM is BAD TIME, as is Wolves: January '84,

19-year-olds Brian Johnson and friend Troy Blakeway are
                                                        jogging,
that they may catch the last bus, after a disco in town.

Leaving the Old Vic Hotel, Wolverhampton, they are pursued by
25 rampaging youths (West Indians, it appears).

Johnson leaps onto a bus but is stabbed twice just as the doors
                                                        close
(two deep long cuts in the thigh, 15 and 12 inches long).

At the Royal Hospital he receives more than seventy stitches.
Blakeway is knifed in the back, trying to flee from the mob –

in the deep 6-inch-long gash he gets thirty stitches; a sobbing
middle-aged parent attends (whose hand a nurse gently pats).

'Very sharp instruments must have been used for making these
nasty
injuries' C.I.D. says (Johnson and Blakeway concur).

It has not been without usefulness that the Press has adminis-
tered
wholesale mad slovenly filth, glibly in apposite prose,

for it has wholly anaesthetized us to what we would either
break under horror of, or, join in, encouraged by trends.

Horrible headlines don't penetrate. Pongoid crania carry
on as though nothing were wrong. *Homo autophagous*, Inc.

**Gillian Weaver aged 22 walking 4-year-old daughter
home when a girl and three men** – hang on, this isn't just *news*:

Gillian Weaver aged 22 walking 4-year-old daughter
home when a girl and three men push her to pavement and steal

£3 from purse – she sits weeping and nursing 4-year-old (let's not
wax sentimental re kids; let's stick to facts, here *are* facts).

As she sits weeping and hugging her daughter, one of the
muggers
comes back and razors her thus **slashes her face 50 times**

(this is the Mirror and not my*self* – I have no axe to grind, right?)
C.I.D. seeks three blacks plus one spotty, ginger-haired white.

Meanwhile, I've gotten the *5-Minute Uke Course* (Guaranteed
Foolproof) –
plinkplinka plinkplinka plonk plinkplinka plinkplinka plonk.

Grans are bewildered by post-Coronation disintegration;
offspring of offspring of *their* offspring infest and despoil.

This is the Age Of The Greatly Bewildered Granny & Grandad,
shitlessly scared by the bad, mindless and jobless and young;

also the Age Of The Dispossessed Young, with nothing to lose by
horribly hurting their sires, babies and cripples, and whose

governments, freely elected and otherwise, function by mores
not altogether removed from their own bestial codes –

those sort of policies, that sort of hardware do not imply much
kindly respect for *H. sap*, mindless and jobless and young . . .

Maybe we're better off under the Civic Centre than up there
what with the LUTEing and that – them inner-cities is BAD,

maybe we're better off here in his WRITINGS, orrible though they
often is sometimes, than THERE – out in that awful real-life

what with its madness and sometimes I thinks the Capting's the only
sane one among the whole lot – Four or five leagues West-sou'west!

Steadily bear away under a reefed lug foresail, ye bilge rats,
synne rises firey and red – sure indycation o' gales,

we have entrapped us a sea-mew and served the blood to ye
                                                        weakest
members of crew, and myself? Liver and heart and ye guts.

42

For accompanying singing, the haunting harmony of the Uke has no superior! Soft summer nights and the Uke are inseparable pals! To wintery jollities the Uke adds zip and sparkle! Too much mystery and confusion have shrouded Uke playing! The Uke is an instrument for the best accompanying of happytime songs! Beautiful and very unusual effects can be achieved! <u>You</u> can learn to play richly harmonious accompaniments *in only a few minutes* by this New Method, and when you have done that **you have accomplished a great deal!**

'This is not Poetry, this is reality, untreated, nasty',
'This is demotic and cheap', 'This is mere caricature',

'This is just relishing violent, nasty . . .' so on and so forth,
Grub St. reviewing its own lame valedictory tosh –

Don't you go brooding and brooding and getting all of a state sir just cos the LITARY GENT don't seem to like your nice books.

Like the old man used to always say 'When we wants YOU to chirp-up, matey, we'll rattle the cage' – don't heed their old tommy-rot.

Grasp the pick lightly between thumb and first finger of right hand. Do not pinch! Move tip of pick back and forth across all four strings. Let that wrist hang loose! Start slow and then increase speed until you produce a smooth, even tone. Well done! The speed you move the pick across the strings will depend on what we call *tempo* (that means *time*) of the number you're accompanying! Well done! **That sounds just dandy!**

These are the questions that Councillors mean to raise at the
                                                              Meeting:
how much promethium remains? Has there been tritium used?

Why did the Army deny there was any contamination?
How do they mean to assure residents no risk remains?

What was the level of contamination? Where had it come from?
What is a 'low level' leak? Why was the public not told?

Why has the Army consistently issued flagrant denials
that any toxin remained after these secret 'events'?

Now you are ready for those oldies we know and love! Yes *Sir*!
Sing, hum, or whistle the tune as you play! Play each chord as
indicated until a new chord is shown. Do not change until you see
another chord indicated! Everyone's just got to join in and **sing
right along there**!

Carrying on as though things were O.K. is what we are good at –
fall-out-proof bunkers are built, orbiting space stations planned.

*Only, it's worse in the papers than what you stick in your writings, what
with I seen a man knocked down WITH MY OWN EYES by black man
and poor soul that was muged was ON CRUTCHES and that is gospel
truth but not as bad as burning baby with CIG END which some swine
done to get purse from mother of two. So even if they are out of work it is
NOT RIGHT they should hurt their own townpeoples. Any road it is too
late now so we can just HOPE FOR BEST which I DO, and will only live
in shelter or outer spaces if there is no other possible. But will NOT eat
sardines morning noon and night.*

Finally now we return to the deep, and reaching our dim craft
drag her black hull through safe shale down to the fathomless
brine.

Next, to the dark-bellied vessel we carry white sails and main-
mast,
lifting aboard her the sheep, white tup and black ewe, and now,

heavily laden with misery, shedding tears in abundance,
hark to our skipper's command, nimble in wit and resource.

Thus we embark while astern of us rise up sail-swelling breezes
surging the blue-prowed ship forth, 12 knots with main-skysail
set.

So, d'ye see, after putting our gear and tackle in order,
all we can do is observe, course set by helmsman and wind.

Thus with full canvas we traverse the waters into ye blackness;
tenebrose, fog-bound, the bar, into the tow of the stream.

Here is perpetual smoke of a city unpierced by sunlight
where ye Cimmerians dwell, unvisible from above.

Here we make fast and drive up from the bilges, bleating, the
stunned sheep
into these bunkers of lead, granite and greyness and stench.

Wend your luff, messmates, and let go the skysail halliards,
mister,
cut the brace pennants and stays, reef the fore-topgallant in,

falling barometer, send down the skysail yard from aloft, sir,
strum with felt pick back and forth, lightly across all four strings,

all sail should be double-gasketted, stow the mainsail and cross-
jack,
make yr pentameters taut: two-and-a-half feet times two,

bend ye now three lower storm-staysails and a storm spanker,
mister,
take in the three upper tops, close-reef the foresail, F sharp,

tighten the B string and place finger at the back of the second
fret of the A string and keep spondees and dactyls close-clewed,

trim yr heroic hexameter (or it may be dactylic),
splice the pentameter aft, finger yr frets as ye go

surely we shouldn't be speaking like this sir, not in Allergic
Dis Talk, taint natural-like: I'm goin back to me prawse

only I've not been old self since they started the TREATMENT but do not
WORRY as they SWEAR it is non malingerent tumer ONLY which
only in my opinion only needs GOOD TONIC and will soon be old self
again but sometimes feeling bit on queer side that is to be expected the
doctor say, but what with one thing and another and the worry over eldest
boy in trouble with LAW I do not know which way to turn but I do
wonder when you read these cases what do the mothers think. and the
father's. because they are all some mothers children which loves them I
should say. Even if they are vilent crimnal. So will soon be back on feet
again but this worry is worrying with internashnal TROUBLE brewing
as the BULLETIN says and I do not feel so perky as previous. So will sign
of for the present

if I could only be just this once pardoned Spawndies and Doctale
which we has never heard of down at the Ten-Storey-Flats.

The Triple Roll is one of the prettiest of all Uke strokes! It is a very simple stroke too, when analyzed! Just follow the simple stages below one step at a time! Soon you will get the 'knack'! Yes *Sir*!

Bring forefinger down across all four strings where neck joins body of Uke. Bring that old fingernail down so that it glides smoothly on the strings. That sounds just swell! Practise this again and again and again! **Then follow with thumb down**. After forefinger leaves last string bring ball of thumb down across strings. **Then bring first finger up**. As thumb leaves last string, bring the ball or fleshy part of forefinger up across all four strings. Yes *Sir*! Forefinger should begin to go up the very second that little old thumb leaves the last string! Say! That sounds like a million dollars! You, good buddy, have just mastered yourself the **TRIPLE ROLL!!!**

I had believed myself fairly inured to foolishness after
6 months for Reuter's in parched mad bloody Lebanon, but

leaving the hotel that morning (with Dickie Pratt, of the Mirror),
in the main street of Sidon, I was presented with this:

out from the shade of the shelled former Admin. Offices stepped
a
miniature, wielding a huge glinting black muzzle and stock,

just as a fat juicy jeep of Israelis swung into vision.
Three or four seconds he stood, sputtering hail at the jeep –

windscreen-glass frosted and one of the front seat occupants
oozed red,
there was a crackle of fire, ten or so seconds, and then,

as from a colander, into the pavement streamed out the juices
of the assailant, a slight soldier/homunculus. Well,

nobody looks for a *motive* from these Old Testament shitters –
thick hate is still in the genes. I learned the boy was aged 12.

Say! At the outset, the beginner may find his fingers just a little bit
stiff and clumsy but this disappears quickly after a little practice!
So why not keep right on along gut-pluck-a-plickin come rain or
come shine! Yes *Sir*! Let's start with the **little finger down** where
the neck joins the body . . .

'Tries to be shocking', 'Predictable, coarse, insensitive,
tasteless . . .'
when I want you to chirp-up, matey, I'll rattle the cage.

Say! What you need to do each day is keep that little old Uke in
tune! Yes *Sir*! Who wants to hear an out-of-tune Uke? That's right!
– Nobody! Say! Why not tune that Uke right now? O.K. let's go!
You need a piano to help you. Tune A string to A on piano. Tune
D string to sound the same as D on piano. Tune F-Sharp string
and B string to sound like those notes on piano. Get it? If you do
not know where these notes are located on piano then ask some
guy who's a pianist to show you. Right?

What with the waiting and not knowing what on earth is the matter
up in the cities and that. Still, it was awful up there

what with last Wednesday that one what married him from the Top Flats
pushing the babby she was, down by the Preesint new shops,

suddenly found erself total surrounded by what-do-you-call-em?
them Rasterfastium blacks; you know, the ones with the LOCKS.

One got er purse but the pleece come and then the LEADER a FAT man
snatched up the babby and STABBED – right in the EYE with a pen,

animals that's what I think of them monsters horrible wild BEASTS
not safe to walk in the streets – not that we could NOW, of course

only it's funny for us being down here under the Civict
Centre – I thought it was all Underground Car Parks and that.

During this voyage ye heavens has been so dree overcast that
no observation by stars, nor yet by sun can be got.

Little round light like a tremulous faint star streams along spark-
ing,
blazes blue, shoots shroud to shroud, running along ye main
yard,

stays half the night with us, settles on fore-shrouds. Spaniards
call it
Fire of St. Elmo – be damned! Fire of ye Devil, it be.

Only the Capting gets mixed up about his time in the Navy –
muddles it up with them YARNS. You know, them ones what you
READ,

not as I'm one for the books and that what with doing the housewort
(no Womans Libbance for ME, what with that much things to do.

get on with THIS Viv and THAT Viv and, well you has to LIVE don't
you?
that's what I think, any road). Close-clew your sails, mates, avast,

shew a reefed foresail to steer by and run for harbour my
buckoes,
oakum discharged from hull's seams; pipe up all hands to the
pumps!

Make ye now ready for Davy Jones, messmates, get ye the
strings tuned,
highest grade sheep's gut, they be – list to the boatman, belay,

as o'er the stream we glide borne by the rolling tide chanting and
rowing . . .
Place your 3rd finger behind 3rd fret of 4th string and strum

Only I've never been happy but what I'm pottering, I ain't –
always the pottering sort, that's why I hates coming DOWN

mind you the Powertree Bloke and the Capting doesn't arf GABBLE –
what with the Capting his YARNS: tother keeps chaingin is VOICE

anyone'd think they was Everyone All Times Everywhere, way they
gabbles and rambles and that: still, they can't help it, poor souls.

Whatsisname says to me 'Viv you're the life and soul of the party' –
Viv, he says, MEANS life, you know (in Greek or Lating or French)

plinkplinka| plinkplinka| plinkplinka| plinkplink| plinkplinka|
plinkplink
plinkplinka| plinkplinka| plonk|| plinkplinka| plinkplinka| plonk

NOTE

KA 007 (p. 17): in September 1983 a Soviet fighter plane shot down a South Korean airliner when all 269 passengers were killed, causing a brief stir.

BOOK II

GOING ON

[Bit of a habit, this feigned indignation,
various forms, Elegiacs, Alcmanics . . .
gets like a game, the old global débâcles.
Just Going On remains possible through the
slick prestidigital art of Not Caring/Hopelessly Caring.]

Muse! Sing the Rasta. who stabbed out a
baby's eye with a Biro
    thereby persuading its mum
    that she should give him her purse

        [Halve the hexameter after three
        dactyls, making it 2 lines;
            halve the pentameter thus –
            this way it fits on the page.]

down in the crazed uriniferous
subway underneath Blake St.
    (leading to Wordsworth Estate)
    spattered with drooled viscid spawl.

        [Squirrelprick Press is producing my
        latest, *Blood Drops in Distich*,
            hand-deckled limp-covered rag,
            Special Edition of ten.]

'Swear by Almighty . . . the evidence
I shall . . . and nothing but the . . .'
 'Sergeant Gillespie, please tell,
 in your own words, to the Court . . .'

'Constable Renton walked into the
charge room just a few moments
 after the time when Carliell
 had been allegedly punched

and he said "I'm sorry, Sarge, but I
caught him one with my ring like.
 Couldn't we sort something out?"
 I said "Get out of the room."

I said "I'm not putting my wife and
kids on the line for you, Renton."
 Carliell had been brought in drunk.'
 'Ladies and gentlemen of . . .

I submit that Mr Carliell was
struck a blow of such vicious . . .
 Call Mr Peter Lee . . . Now,
 you, on the night of . . . next cell . . .

tell the Court, please Mr Lee, what you
heard that night in the next cell.'
 'I could hear screaming, and he
 shouted "You've knocked out my eye.

Why have you done this?" he shouted, and
I could hear him like screaming . . .'
 'Constable Renton is charged,
 ladies and gentlemen of . . .'

I am traduced in the press (for a
poem weary of war-rent
    mad bloody Lebanon) as
    Antisemitic, Bad Hat.

No, no, not antisemitic, dears,
antibutchery only;
    both sides still deadlocked in hate,
    sanguin'ry as the O.T.

Literal Readers, Perverse Exe-
gesists bay for my spilt blood . . .
    Wait till the lit. mags. unleash
    my controversial next op. –

Muse!, sing the family *Strigidae*
hooting 'hooey' and 'hooey'
    down in a dell in the dark.
    Hooey and hooey and tosh.

['. . . you will not know me but . . . something in
common . . . both up at Oxford . . .
        six years your junior – yet
        both of us Balliol men!. . .']

All of you goat-esses be not so
Frisky, lest the bold he-goat
*   Rouseth himself to ye all!*
*   Muses, begin the sweet song.*

['. . . so my dear Lockhart I venture to
send these "Lyrical Fragments
        Done Into English" in case
        "Quarterly" readers may care . . .']

If 'tis your fancy to fasten your
Cloak-end on your right shoulder,
*   And you can stand an attack,*
*   Get thee to Egypt forthwith.*

We all grow grey at the temples and
Time's snow creeps down our cheek-bones;
*   We should be active while sap*
*   Courses yet fresh in our joints.*

['. . . Sir, I remain Yr. Obedient
Servant, Reverend Wolly,
        Parsonage, May '35,
        Claresmould-cum-Cowperly, Snotts.']

Eunica mocked me when I would have
Kissed her; then did she spit thrice
*   Into her bosom and said*
*   'Neatherd, thy stench is obscene'.*

Deborah Fallon, aged 19, is
handcuffed hugging an oak tree,
   forced by Rats Chapter to watch
   boyfriend (D. Cox, 22)

stabbed to death frenziedly, during which
she screams, pleads for her own life,
   but she is told she must die
   (strangled to death with a scarf).

This is because the Rats Chapter from
London ordered the killing
   (part of a scheme to 'sort out'
   Lucifer's Outlaws – a new

Northampton Chapter of Angels who
have been grassing about the
   whereabouts of an arms cache).
   Fallon and Cox are bumped off.

Serjeant-at-Arms (Stephen Parkinson)
and the President (Michael
   Bardell) of Lucifer's lot
   have been instructed to 'waste'

Fallon and Cox and, to indicate
that the Chapter has done it,
   they must slice one of her tits
   off and unpeel her scant pants . . .

[Which elegiacs aren't merely for
silly miscreant Angels,
   but all *H. sap* gone berserk –
   finished pernicious mad shits.]

'I am delighted to see that the
front page carries a photo
     of Douglas Fairbanks, the *dear*;
     I must have seen all his films,

younger and happier days, my boy,
younger, happier times when –'
     'No no no, Granny dear, no,
     this is no movie, but *real*:

"Prisoner threatens to murder a
hostage", this is the caption,
     "during the riot last week,
     Sexto gaol, Lima, Peru – " '

'Such a fine actor, dear boy, but I
can not think from which picture
     they can have taken that snap.
     Is it a pirate rôle, dear?'

'Gran, dearest Gran, this is *not* Douglas
Fairbanks cast as a pirate
     (or cast as anything else);
     this is a *prisoner*, see?

Listen, I'll read you the –' 'Oh such a
dashing figure he was though,
     I saw them all, you know, all,
     what I liked best was the one –'

' "Prisoners threatened to kill all the
hostaged lawyers, officials
     and other prisoners, if
     they were not given a safe

conduct and transport from gaol, and a
29-year-old woman
     (un-named) had first degree burns
     after the prisoners poured

petrol all over her, set her on
fire and watched as she –" ' 'Dear boy,
  I have remembered, of course,
  silly of me to forget!

This must be out of his picture of
'26, *The Black Pirate*.
  Oh, such a wonderful film,
  such a young thing I was, then.'

' "One of the hostages died after
being shot in the stomach –" '
  'He was a ladies' man, dear,
  oh such a ladies' man, yes.'

' "One of the victims was injured when
Sexto prisoners tried to
  cut off his legs with a saw –" '
  'Or could it be *Robin Hood*?

What was the date of dear *Robin Hood*,
darling? Dashing, so dashing.'
  ' "Statements from some of the guards
  say that an inmate cut out

one female hostage's tongue (she was
Carmen Montes, a typist)
  after she answered by phone
  questions put her by the press –" '

'No dear, I do not think somehow that
Mr Fairbanks was ever
  featured in *Carmen* at all.
  You are mistaken, dear boy.'

' "One of the victims, who worked at the
prison, Mr Rodolfo
  Farfan, was shot at point blank
  range in the abdomen and

slumped on his knees on a balcony
right in front of police and
    pressmen when inmates' demands
    (they wanted getaway vans)

met with refusal and –" ' 'Certainly,
dear, it *is The Black Pirate*,
    such a swashbuckling romp.
    More devilled kidneys, dear boy?'

Granny had been in the hospital
ever since she went funny.
    She was OK in herself –
    they made her do little things.

Each week some Volunteer Ladies came
(just to help with the Occu-
    pational Therapy) and
    very nice ladies they were.

This week the Volunteer Ladies were
making Grandmother bake scones;
    then, with a nice cup of tea,
    they let her gum one, still warm,

golden-brown luxury, scrumptiously
melting thickly-spread butter.
    Oh, she had always loved scones.
    This was her best treat for years.

Coroner Crawford-Clarke said that her
food had lodged in her larynx.
    'This would bring on very quick
    sudden death.' I ate the rest.

In City Centre it were [you will
notice Regional Accent
    tweely denoted by quaint
    phrasing] me sister were there

visiting like, an er lad as is
nearly seven were took short –
    needed to go to the bog.
    Well, Public Toilets was near,

so er just took im along to em
but they couldn't use *Ladies*
    (where er could look arter im)
    cos there were queue like outside.

So er sends im in nex door like to
Gents as seemed to be empty.
    Well, e seemed gorn a long time;
    so, when some feller comes by,

er says Just take a look in please an
see if nipper's OK like.
    So this bloke goes in you know.
    Sudden-like, out runs three youths

 – what they ad done were to stuff the kid's
mouth with bog-paper roll then
    cut with a penknife is poor
    little dick orf and is balls.

Justice was seen to be done in South
Africa yesterday, thanks to
    laudable Judge Irving Steyn
    sitting in Rand Supreme Court.

Mr Francisco Quintino, a
56-year-old white man,
    shot dead a very bad rogue
    (called Macks Lerutia, a black)

whom he saw stealing the milk money
(63 cents) from a doorstep
    in the suburban all-white
    neighbourhood where he resides.

Judge Irving Steyn cleared Francisco of
all the charges against him.
    Also, sagacious Judge Steyn
    said how Francisco 'deserved

some sort of medal for what he had
done' and praised him for having
    selflessly acted – he said
    this was a real 'Civic Deed'.

Also, His Honour applauded the
'public service' which this Fran-
    cisco Quintino had done –
    curbed the unfortunate rash,

recently noted, of Milk Money
Thefts from decent white suburbs.
    (63 cents is about
    35 pence, English cash.)

Sadist Girl Guide Susan Hardwick and
boyfriend, 22-year-old
   Walsall man Martin Downes, robbed
   Mabel France (75).

Hardwick befriended the 'trusting old
fireman's widow' by running
   errands and doing odd jobs.
   Later, she 'relished' how Downes

put Mabel France through a 'wicked, per-
sistent, year's degradation'.
   Downes told the police he was 'skint',
   Mabel was 'just a good con'.

Those in the court heard accounts of how
Downes had burned the old lady
   using his cigarette-end,
   then had rubbed salt in the wounds.

Sometimes he fastened her eyes closed with
clothes-pegs, making her sit still*
   hour after hour after hour,
   whimpering, frightened and hurt.

One day he tortured, then set loose, a
rat, which bit her; another
   (this was perhaps his most famed
   highly original trick),

he took a toilet brush, whipped up the
widow's skirts and performed – well,
   what, rather coyly, the court
   called an 'indecent assault'.

*Often, it was alleged, with a plastic carnation stuck up her nose.

Often he forced her to swallow huge
doses of laxative tablets;
    she shat incontinently
    (Hardwick thought this was dead great).

Sometimes he plagued the old woman with
'phantom' voices he claimed were
    those of her husband and son
    (both of whom had been long dead).

£600 and her wedding ring
had been stolen and squandered.
    Mabel was too scared to tell
    police of the year-long ordeal.

Poor Martin wept uncontrollably
as his sentence was read out
    (4 years they gave him, and Sue
    got 6 months youth custody).

[. . . page after page of trite news reports
rehashed, vomiting squalor.
    Over-exposure to vile
    madness (from verse or the box)

makes for immunity. None of the
ghastly nasties he re-spews
    eases or mends with the mere
    telling *again* of its filth.]

Si señor, sure we har claiming the
bomb as Glorious Blow by
    Forces of Liberate Dark
    Dictate Oppression. Too long

far have we, fathers and hrandfathers
forced to Slavery lifes hwich
    Army of Liberate fight
    struggles till all mens are dead!

Down with the generalísimo!
(not the present or last hwon,
    only the hwon pefore last),
    Viva la Muerte! señor,

Viva el excelentísimo
Señor conde de Torre-
    gamberro! Yes sirs my friend,
    what is the matter that some

dies for the Cause of the hwons that is
thinking right in this matters?
    This she's Political's War.
    Sure what are some person lifes?

We not Guerrillas amigo but
Counter-Anti-Guerrilla
    them was our Leaders but now –
    those is our Enemy, si,

ow you say por favor now they has
showed False Ideologics.
    Terrorist Actions too bad;
    this why we take such Campaigns!

This very Positive Actions she
may have kill some who have no
    doings with Rebels but so?
    Bombs she not go off for fun.

Don't say amigo you not with the
understandings of why we
    fights in montañas of South?
    This are the struggles to death!

OK so 20 am dead and some
shrapnels goes to some peoples –
    we har of People's own blood!
    This is of why we shall fight!

Last bomb was not our bomb *that* was bomb
blown hwen Traitor who carries
    gets it hexplosure too soon
    killing himself and some mans.

Somehow you get mix up, señor, you
see we Neutral in all thing
    this hwy the reasons hwe fights!
    Freedoms to Govermans Farce!

Same Costa Rica but also with
Nicaraguan Border!
    Now you mus hunderstand well
    which why this bombs must hexplode.

Just hypothermia (Coroner
for St. Pancras announces)
    caused this particular death.
    5-year-old Elliot Hinds'

mum and her boyfriend were said to have
got the idea from watching
    some late-night film on T.V.
    Anyway, Elliot died.

What he had done was to wet the bed
(that most heinous of child crimes)
    so, his mum's boyfriend took charge –
    held the boy under a shower

(full on the 'Cold' setting) for about
15 minutes. It seems that
    'Elliot usually screamed
    while being given cold showers'.

Sagely, the Coroner's jury re-
turns the old 'Misadventure'.
    'Ankle, I have little doubt,
    not through vindictiveness, but

probably just out of some way of
trying to discipline this lad,
    latched on to this form of cure.'
    (¼ hour's icy-cold shower.)

So, the Director of Public
Prosecutions decides that
    there is *not* gross negligence;
    therefore no Manslaughter charge.

Burning, per contra, is equally
efficacious in these things –
   30-year-old Terence Rose
   stoutly denied G.B.H.

Julie, his wife, though, explained how he
held their 2-year-old daughter
   '2 inches from the gas fire.
   It was full on' she alleged.

'Tara was screaming and tried to pro-
tect her legs with her hands, but
   he took no notice of her.
   Screaming and squirming she was.'

Some minutes later she 'messed on the
floor' and Terence informed her
   she was a 'dirty young bitch'.
   Mrs Rose told how he then

went for the slipper and hit the burnt
bottom and, as he smacked her
   'her flesh flew up in the air'
   (blistered, from burning, you see).

One night, about six weeks afterwards,
Terence went to the girl's room.
   Tara had peed in the bed.
   Terence was very annoyed.

Mrs Rose told how he 'called her a
dirty cow and I heard him
   dragging her into the loo.
   I heard him 26 times –

I heard him smacking her 26
times with the slipper. Her bottom'
  (still burnt) 'was bleeding' she said.
  Scars are still visible now.

[Clearly, then, some of us entertain
scant regard for the kiddies;
  ditto the kiddies for us –
  malice reciprocal, dread.]

'Outraged of Telford' has written to
tell the Editor how, last
    Saturday, she and her spouse
    went to the Precinct to shop.

There was 'a group of young teenagers
lounging round in a doorway'
    spawling and picking their spots.
    One, a girl aged about 12,

moved from her mates to the side of the
old chap (husband of 'Outraged'),
    where she took hold of his arm,
    disgorged her pink bubble-gum,

said to him 'What do you think of the
youth of Telford, eh, sexy?'
    'Not very much', he replied,
    shaking her free of his arm.

Whereupon she became violent,
spat phlegm into the man's face,
    screamed 'Well I'll tell you what, cunt,
    we think *you're* old fucking shits!'

('Outraged of Telford' has written it
c dash t, for discretion;
    similarly f dash g;
    similarly s dash t.)

[As I have elsewhere remarked, these are
times which baffle the oldies –
    wee kiddiwinkies infest,
    parricide, parricide soon . . .]

[This isn't elegy but
   thanksgiving; therefore invert –
place the pentameter first and the
hymn/hexameter after.]

   April – the Met. Office says
   warmest since records began.
Pure cerulean of sky and, be-
hind the cottage, thick-fleeced ewes

   suckle robust new Clun lambs,
   celandines gleam from sunned turf,
first of the season's *Phylloscopus*
warblers *hweet* from the pleached thorn,

   primrose – [enough of this crap.
   Sounds like the Plashy Fen School.
No *list* of species can ever be
more than gross insult to them –

   patronized tweely by bards
   (awfully keen on Wild Life)].
I shall confine myself merely to
bringing forth a scrubbed table,

   setting it down in lush grass,
   placing rich wallflowers, just cut,
fumous of uncloying honey, and
to the business of olives,

   watercress, paprika, rice,
   breaking moist pizza apart
(anchovies, capers and sharp oreg-
ano bruised into fragrance),

   sloshing out goblets of light
   sap-green cool Tokay d'Alsace,
cascading Vichy, bright sparkle of
glassfuls frosted to fjord-cold . . .

[All he could do was *report*
horrible and (some) nice things.]
There is an impotent gratitude
goes with godless well-being.

Elsewhere, the world is to-cock;
here though, quite simply, this hour
glows as amongst the most joyful (old-
fashioned word) in a short life.

Mr Mugabe had kindly ar-
ranged a Government tour for
   journalists, that we might see
   with our own eyes and report

how Ndebele tribe villagers
had *not* suffered abuses
   from his nice CIO* men
   (30 of whom came along,

armed to the teeth, with us then as a
guard of honour, unwanted),
   how allegations were 'False,
   spread by alarmists and foes'.

This Ndebele supports oppos-
ition leader Nkomo;
   get my drift, see what I mean?
   Witnesses, then, were few/brave.

One Dr Devee reported how
he had treated a hundred
   patients who said they were raped,
   beaten or had their kin shot.

One Ndebele explained how he
watched troops gun down his brother
   whom they had forced to help dig,
   screaming for mercy, his grave.

One witness said 'I am not afraid –
there are too many have been
   beaten and, yes, that includes
   small babies on women's backs.

*Zimbabwe PM Robert Mugabe's Central Intelligence Organization.

Six were shot dead by the soldiers – I
know, I handled the bodies.'
  (CIO officers took
  photographs of this young man;

maybe they paid him a social call
later on in the evening.)
  Witnesses showed us a wood
  where there were two mounds of earth.

These, they alleged, were the places where
six men, killed by Mugabe's
  troops, had been piled in a tump
  roughly gone over with dirt.

Villagers In Matabeleland
Tell Of Killing & Rape By –
  [Who wants to dwell on it all?
  Nil Carborundum, OK?

What after Elegy? Callous de-
tatchment feigning concern for
  Post-Elegiac and Post-
  Post-Elegiac *H. sap* . . .

Shake off those gloomy and old-fangled
boring, sad Elegiacs!
  Try our own new-look re-vamped
  Alcmanic Strophe, wherein

  form, ham-philosophy, alcoholism
  may not *transcend*, but do celebrate simply
  just Going On, Getting On With It. Try our
fun Catalectic Tetrameter, with Hexameter added!]

These are the days of the horrible headlines,
Bomb Blast Atrocity, Leak From Reactor,
Soccer Fans Run Amock, Middle East Blood Bath,
PC Knocks Prisoner's Eye Out In Charge Room.
Outside, the newsvendors ululate. Inside,
lovers seek refuge in succulent plump flesh,
booze themselves innocent of the whole shit-works.
Why has the gentleman fallen face-forward
into his buttered asparagus, Garçon?
He and his girlfriend have already drunk two
bottles of Bollinger and they were half-tight
when they arrived at the place half-an-hour since.
Waiters man-handle the gentleman upright,
aim him (with smirks at the lady) towards his
quails (which he misses and slumps in the gravy –
baying, the while, for 'Encore du Savigny').
He is supplied with the Beaune, which he noses,
quaffs deeply, relishes . . . sinks to the gingham
where he reposes susurrantly. There is
'63 Sandeman fetched to revive him.
Chin on the Pont l'Evêque, elbow in ash-tray,
as from the *Book of the Dead*, he produces
incomprehensible hieroglyphs, bidding
Access surrender the price of his coma
unto the restaurateur, kindly and patient.
These are the days of the **National Health Cuts**,
days of the end of the innocent liver;
they have to pay for it privately, who would seek anaesthetic.

['There is a Madness abroad, and at home the
cities run bloody with Riot; my children,
know yourselves happy who, far from base Commerce,
plough your own acreage. Pray for all Statesmen.
Though we had nothing to do with them, we must
suffer for Sins of our sires . . .' My poor flock will
be unaware of Horatian echoes
when I deliver this to them on Sunday –
two or three scarcely forbearing to slumber.
There is a Madness abroad – in Retirement only, is Saneness.]

Sweet-voicèd holy-tongued maidens [quoth Alcman],
My limbs can no longer carry me. Would that
I could go, be as the Kingfisher who doth
Go with his mates on the flower of the billow,
Height of foam having rejoicing heart sea-dark bird very sacred!

[Far from the clash of arms, having the cure of
Claresmould-cum-Cowperly, all I can hope is
these humble fragments translated may lighten
some reader's heart, as my own is disburthened
daily engaging in, if futile, harmless
little unhurtful things. So, 'My Dear Lockhart . . .
whether the Lyrica Graeca here Englished
may be of interest to "Quarterly" readers . . .
Sir, I remain yr. most . . .' There is a Madness currently ram-
pant.]

Has been ordainèd three seasons, the Summer,
Winter, and Autumn the third one, and fourthly
Spring when things sprout or are lush but one can not,
You can not, it is not possible that one,
Eats to or feeds to satiety, fullness . . .
These words and song were invented, composed by,
Alcman-found, putting together the prolix,
Chattering noisiness utterance of some
Partridges . . . [There is a Madness abroad and elsewhere
confusion.

81

Madness abroad. Through the Parsonage casement,
(cawing for carrion) crows; from the stable,
audible hiss of the groom at the pale roan;
moan of the ancient yew under whose umbrage
rest the dear bones of my good predecessors.
Ah, but, odds-heartikins! How late the hour – the Up Mail
already!]

I don't know quite how it come about, but that
night I was utterly pissed as a – well I'd
been on the bottles of Special since half-past
five when they opened and then a few whiskies.
All I remember is puking and then the Hurry-Up-Waggon.

It was the usual set-up of two rough
blankets, a mattress and bog in the corner
(stunk of stale piss cos the flusher was nackered),
normal graffiti scratched on the green bedstead,
'Coppers is bastards' was wrote and I added
'Just do your bird like a man and stop moanin.'
If you stood up on your toes you could just see
through the bars over the yard to the charge room's clock on the
green wall.

Then I hears this bloke what come in with my batch,
pissed he was, also like, screamin and screamin
'You've knocked my eye out!' and 'Why have you done this?'
They done the copper what done it at Southwark –
I had to go and give evidence (I got
pissed as a rat for the Hell of it, after that little session).

Aping the brash U.S. varsities, silly
Regional Arts men are buying the local
poetry-wallah's Rough Manuscript Draft Sheets –
'Rough Drafts' belong in the wastepaper-basket
(one might as well propose purchasing Fleming's dirty old test-
tubes).

dear sir and Maderm

> *I thought I would write as*
> *not wrote for SOME TIME account of the ILLNES*
> *What with the Gennal Electioned and suchlike*
> *voting the various Pollertics peoples*
> *me and the husband has gone to the pole – well*
> *ought to go shouldn't you as it is RIGHTS like*
> *only I must say you wonder like sometimes*
> *why they wont do what the voters are wanting.*
> *such as no war and more Schools and the Pension.*
> *my man has WUOND from the last which is horrid*
> *only he say they should BAN the atomics*
> *as it is FUTIL he say, but we dont know*
> *being just voters which isnt the same as*
> *Guverning which is for those who are GOOD BRAINS*
> *out of the BIG unerversity College*
> *but it seem sometimes the pollertick MPs*
> *does not do Sensible things like to spend on*
> *Aerocraft MISILS that kill some poor peoples*
> *where they are DROP. but we only are voters*
> *which cannot KNOW like the Goverment peoples*
> *what is best but American peoples*
> *seems to be feared at the RUSSHA invadings*
> *so we must have them. the Rockits. but sometimes*
> *maybe I wonders and so does the HUSBAND*
> *what will INVADING FORS get if it comes here?*
> *what with no money for SCHOOL or the old folks?*
> *only we cannot know what they are thinking.*
> *MPs and suchlikes PRY MINISTERS as they*
> *KNOW more than we do. so must be the leaders*
> *therefor we just do the best we can manige*
> *Only the SON who the police is arrested*
> *who is GOOD LAD but they say he is MUGGER*
> *oh dear I do not know which way to turn but*
> *still love my boy who is GOOD BOY to Mother*
> *even if crimaly wrong to the lawyers*
> *How to stop vilence and crime and the warfair*
> *that is the questions what faces the whole WORLD*
> *goverments nowdays and what is the answer*

I dont know nor does the HUSBAND we only
have to get on with it just GOING ON is
all we can do in the present situation
which is why I do the Cleaning for people
so that the husband which CANT WORK account of
wuond from LAST WAR that is v. painful sometimes
also the kiddies can live and be happy
even the one that is jailed (when he come out)
he must be looked after even though some say
he is bad boy. I say I am the MOTHER
so I must love him like all the worlds peoples
even if sometimes is HORRIBLE must make BEST OF A BAD JOB

hoping it finds you as leave me Yrs Faithly. VIV keep yr chin up!

When they were chasing the 'Most Wanted Gunman',
every day everyone looked in the paper
(Elsie, the barmaid, used always to leave the
Sun on the counter for regulars) and we
all there considered that he was a bastard –
dangerous bastard who wouldn't mind using
guns on the police or the public, a nutter.
'Sooner they ration that bastard to H.M. porridge the better.'

Everyone knew him to be a prize bastard
'Bloody good job' I remarked to the Lounge when
plain-clothes-men cornered him down in the Tube and
all of us then if we'd half a chance would have
strung-up the dangerous lunatic dirty bastard but, mind you,

25 years is a terrible
prospect, if you love someone.
    They believe he was obsessed
    with getting back to his girl

(can't blame him, either, for that – she was
very sexy the Sun said).
    He wrote her desperate notes
    like: 'All I have now is death . . .

take away pain of my not being
with you' that sort of garbage.
    'What ever death is, it can't
    be worse than waiting for you.'

Cold in his T-shirt and underpants
with a piece of electric
    flex from a fridge round his neck;
    desolate poor little bloke.

This is unclean: to eat turbots on Tuesdays,
tying the turban unclockwise at cockcrow,
cutting the beard in a south-facing mirror,
wearing the mitre whilst sipping the Bovril,
chawing the pig and the hen and the ox-tail,
kissing of crosses with peckers erected,
pinching of bottoms (except in a yashmak),
flapping of cocks at the star-spangled-banner,
snatching the claret-pot off of the vicar,
munching the wafer without genuflexion,
facing the East with the arse pointing backwards,
thinking of something a little bit risqué,
raising the cassock to show off the Y-fronts,
holding a Homburg without proper licence,
chewing the cud with another man's cattle,
groping the ladies – or gentry – o'Sundays,
leaving the tip on the old-plum-tree-shaker,
speaking in physics instead of the Claptrap,
failing to pay due obeisance to monkeys,
loving the platypus more than the True Duck,
death without Afterlife, smirking in Mecca,
laughing at funny hats, holding the tenet
how that the Word be but fucking baloney,
failing to laud the Accipiter which Our Lord saith is Wisdom.

Started by *Australopithecus*, these are
time-honoured Creeds (and all unHoly doubters
shall be enlightened by Pious Devices:
mayhems of tinytots, low-flying hardwares,
kneecappings, letterbombs, deaths of the firstborns,
total extinctions of infidel unclean wrong-godded others).

Atheist bigoted bad taste . . . [well, yes but,
unlike the worst of the killing religions,
this doesn't seek to do physical harm to other-believers.]

Smugly it advocates going on sanely
tendering love at a personal level . . .
[yes, there's a smugness and paradox to that
love which discriminates Sweetheart and Swinehound;
'Love me, love my madness' – non-acquiescent embracing, it
should be.]

This is the verse of negation and sterile
rage; the ironic/sarcastic declines to
nihilist cynical mute acquiescence . . .
[nihilist, certainly, so it is. But to
recognize isn't to acquiesce. Sterile, angry the *OIMOI!*]

Green-painted steel truckle, mattress besmirched with
previous occupants' greasy exudings
(2 blankets ditto), unflushable toilet
smelling (like privet flowers) sickly of urine,
unctuous phlegm-green wall, floor of smoothed concrete,
meshed fenestration, unfunctioning bell-push,
ferric inspection-plate slid tight in oiled slots.

Lysosomes, ribosome, sac, cytoplasm,
sausage-shaped small mitochondria, membrane,
smooth endoplasmic reticulum (lipid
molecules), globular ribosomes on the
rough endoplasmic reticulum (proteins),
nucleus storing genetic instruction
programmed in deoxyribonucleic . . .

[Inside the cramped cell, the coded graffito:
Just do your bird like H. sap *without moaning.*]

[Letter to Lockhart: '. . . Alcmanium Metrum
may be of interest to "Quarterly" readers;
and I must hope that "The Scorpion" shall not
look with disfavour upon these slight, Englished,
little, unhurtful things. Sir, I remain yr . . .']

I know the Laws (or the musical modes or
Strains or the customs) of all of the winged tribe.

Ah, it is not Aphrodite but manic
Eros who plays at the games which a child will –
Caning a-down on the tips of the flowers,
Blooms of the sweet-smelling **Cyperus** *marsh plant;*
And do not, blooms of this, contact or touch me!

Peaks and the clefts of the mountains are sleeping,
Headlands and torrents, and crawling tribes (which are
Fed by the loamy black), animals of the
Mountain and race of the bees and the brute-beasts
Inside the deeps of the purple sea. They sleep
Also the tribes of extended attenuated or long-wings.

[Theme for the sermon at Claresmould o'Sunday:
'. . . visit the sins of the fathers upon the . . .
unto the third and the fourth generation . . .'
There is, odds-beddikins!, madness abroad, and
something horrendous seems likely to happen,
newspaper print blackens palms with the world's dirt,
Terrible Lizards* are being awoken –
daily the saurian monsters are raised and Genesis threatened.

All I can hope is for solace in these poor impotent strophes.]

*The nomenclature *Dinosauria* was established at the 1841 Plymouth
meeting of the British Association for the Advancement of Science.

There is a reciprocity here of maniac malice.
   Theists are butchers, and twerpish their god-loves,
   vicious PC punches prisoner's eye out,
   Angels euphorically slaughter their buddies,
   some PMs have Special Men to do-in your
   Mrs or nipper or you if you vote wrong,
   kiddies are calling us cunts and will kill us,
   addle-brained Counter-revs. maim all and sundry,
   man sets to work on his neighbour with rip-saw,
   horrified mum watches mugger stab tot blind,
   niggers are here to be murdered in season,
OAP women are here to be fucked with lavatory brushes,
my little baby annoys me – I burn it, punch off the blisters.

   [Bit of a habit, the feigned indignation,
   various metres, Alcmanics and so forth,
   ludic responses to global débâcles.
   Just Going On remains possible through the
slick prestidigital art of Not Caring/Hopelessly Caring.]

Half-batty Writer-in-Residence meets the
totally lunatic amateur hopefuls
gathered in Scumton Community Centre
proffering Fictional Openings e.g.

(1)

I won't forget in a hurry the time Young
Master came home on a Saturday *sober*:
dog didn't know him and bit him, the old mare
whinnied and cast off a shoe, and the Mistress
swooned clean away at the novelty of it.

(2)

Sappy, the Last Man, was whistling Nielsen's
4th when his dungarees started to smoulder.

[**Poets' & Novelists' Surgery** – ballocks.
Still, I suppose, if it keeps them from other, more harmful
mischief . . .]

Ten million million kilometres are 1
light year (approx.), and at 2¼
million light years lies the most distant object
dimly apparent to *sapiens* vision
i.e. Andromeda Galaxy (nearby
M33 is at 2.4 million
light years, but only perceptible given ideal conditions).

You no love Elephant, Islam, Jehovah?
You no love Christ, Kakistocracy, Kali?
You no love Crapicrap Mightiest Monkey?
You no bow down to the Moon, to the UFO?
You no love balderdash? You no love daft hats?
You no love thuribles? [You no love puny
arrogant cowardly grasping at transcendentalist bunkum?]
We send you envelopes full of our faeces.
We send you Jiffy bags – blow-up your faces.
We send the tanks and the rockets [because the
Prophet saith blast us to buggery, in his Infinite Wisdom].

Here are the frail astronomically puny
half way through ten billion years of a sun life –
four million tonnes of its matter per second
warming them/cooling it. All suns collapsing,
dense cores imploding towards tiny compact
white dwarfs or neutron stars, pulsars or black holes.
Frail astronomical punies who need not
further exacerbate grim molestations
already programmed in impartial light years,
cosmic vicissitudes, cooling expansion;
no need to bugger *each other* up further –
all hands susceptible anyway to the old astral physics.

You got a purse full of dollars and me not.
You got a mansion with stuff in what I want.
You like the football team what isn't my one.
You wear the scarf what is not the right colours.
You got a body not want me to stuff it.
You ugly oldster got pension. Me take it.
Smash in your faces with head-butts and crowbars.
Rip down your knickers at knife-point and snatch it.
Splinter the bottles and slash till the blood comes.
[Dominant morphisms hatch on the terraces dripping with apes'
                                                    gore.]

My work is closely allied to the 'Double
Quasar' (so-called) at some 10 000 million
light years from this planet. Like many quasars,
this has a couple of radio lobes which
stretch out some one hundred thousand, or so, light
years. It's a more or less average quasar,
lying, I say, at some 10 000 million light years away from

Don't get excited about it – it's only
updated *Australopithecus* and you
can't talk about it (or be it) without ac-
cepting what characterizes a species,
can't profess fondness or caring for *it* ab-
stract from its coded behavioural special characteristics.

That's what they are, the old daft superstitious
killing religions and butcherous greedy
national/personal unlovely snatchings,
sapiens attributes as are the brilliant
radiotelescopes, bio-tech, hi-tech.
(Here is invented Obscurity, wherefrom
triumphs invented Discovery; blinding
privileged Revelation where there had been no concealment.)

Love it, love its fossil skull-splitting cudgel,
love it, love its anti-tank-grenade-launcher,
love it, love its neo-pongoid theological tenets.

[Yet I persist in this unhelpful habit,
sham, atavistic, unwanted, indulgent.
Thirty-four years since the death of John Lockhart . . .,
still I can scarcely forbear to address him
(not that he printed my Lyrica Graeca
ever, alas, in his 'Quarterly' pages –
feeble Alcmanics I seem to recall then
proffering unto him . . ., equally weakly,
doubtless, these graspings at dignity through my
crude adaptation of Alcaeus' metric
into sad English beyond Elegiac . . .
In an old form is there dignity yet there?).
Ha! I am foundering, as is my Nation – Ocean o'erwhelms us.]

Now we must drunk and drink with a will we must,
Force or a zest since dead now is Myrsilus.
   [Somehow I feel I have not captured
      quite what the beautiful fragment once was.

I have derived from Alcaeus' metrical
four-line invention; twisted to travesty,
   rudely reduced to dactyls, spondees,
      quantity ousted by Englished stressing.]

State of the four winds I do not comprehend!
One wave is at us, rolling from gunwale there,
   One from the other, we in centre,
      Carried around in the black ship, hard pressed

By the great tempest; sea (or bilge) filling the
Hole for the mainmast; now all the sailcloth is
   Ragged with rent holes, holy, hole-rent,
      Great rips all over it, torn shards, sail-rips.

[Tūm-tĕe-tĕe|tūm-tūm‖tūm-tĕe-tĕe| tūm-tĕe-tĕe
Tūm-tĕe-tĕe|tūm-tūm‖ tūm-tĕe-tĕe| tūm-tĕe-tĕe
  Tūm-tĕe-tĕe| tūm-tūm‖tūm-tūm| tūm-tūm
    Tūm-tĕe-tĕe| tūm-tĕe-tĕe| tūm-tūm tūm-tūm.]

Poverty: painful, also un-bearable!
Poorness is Evil, bringing great peoples down
  Onto their knee-caps, kneeling, bowed down.
    Comes also Helplessness, Poorness' sister.

[I am as worn, indeed, as the century.
Gone is my joy – in Crimea's carnages,
  year in which Lockhart joined his Maker,
    (tortuous, ánachronistic stanzas)

there fell my loins' dear fruit under Cardigan.
Blasphemous, that book, five autumns afterwards,
  burst on us even here in Claresmould –
    terribly credible, Adam ape-born.]

Jupiter drizzles; out of the Heaven comes
Great storm or tempest; streams of the waters are
  Frozen-up. Cast off (strike down) tempest,
    Poke the fire, mix the wine, honey'd, don't stint.

[Reverend Webb has found a new Nebula,
'N.G.C. Two Nought Two Seven'*, so he said,
  earnestly, over Malmsey last night.]
    Wine is man's telescope [quoth Alcaeus].

*NGC 7027 (not 2027) had been thought to be a star until, in 1879, the Reverend T.W. Webb discerned its slightly elongated shape. It was included in Johan Dreyer's New General Catalogue of Nebulae and Clusters of Stars (1888).

What are these birds come? Far from the (or from the
Bounds of the) Ocean? Dapple-necked, having-stripes,
  Tribe of the long-wings? [Long-wings, long-wings . . .
    Ah! But a tireful lacuna halts me.]

Reps and execs in *Plastics* and *Packaging*
(holiday-wise it's Costa del Parvenu),
   Fitments and *Fords*, complete Expenses
     Forms for their Beer'n'Byte basket scampi.

They are disgusting; I am a secular
saint of the breed Empiricist Atheist
   (here is a quid for Oxfam hapless
     starving in sewer-pipes somewhere beastly).

There was a scuffle and shouts on the
station concourse and then they
    ran out and I heard a knife
    drop on the floor and three men

ran off and there was a terrified
Rastafarian lying
    bleeding like mad from the chest.
    Railway men gave him first aid

but he continued to bleed from a
gaping gash in the rib cage.
    Gently I rested his frizzed
    head in my arm like a girl's.

  One of the officers taking my statement
said how he died in the hospital later,
how he was wanted for mugging, and not to
waste too much sympathy brooding on someone
equally capable, probably, of the same sort of slaughter.

    Being thus fully conscious of hideous
    qualities in us (knowing these qualities,
        merely specific, are not 'special'
            other than to ourselves) does not mean an

    overall hate for, nor acquiescence in,
    sapiens wholesale. Even its butcherous
        lunatic scum is (oimoi!) part it –
            love it (with its bloody cleaver)/loathe it.

Media elbow-deep in the offal-bin
(Flensed-Alive MPs Mangled In Bomb-Attack),
nincompoop zealots toy with jelly,
Crass Kakistocracies viva, viva . . .

Moisturize lungs with juice of the vinous-bred,
Sirius rises, now is the difficult
  Season of hardness, all are thirsty
    Out of the terrible heat the hotness.

Grasshopper (sweetly) goes into mourning, now
Makes an annoying sound from the foliage;
  Artichoke now is thornful blooming,
    Women are utterly most foul, ghastly

Tribe of Mankind is impotent (delicate,
Helplessly unpeeled, wasted to weakliness),
  Sirius parches, not just head but
    (Organs of genesis) knee-caps also.

But let there be a garland of aniseed
Coiling around my twisted and wrinkled neck,
  Also let sweet myrrh be poured over
    Onto my (over our) chest or bosom.

[Garnering remnants, fossilized, civilized,
I, mealy-mouthed disruptor of harmonies,
  strive in an old form (not strong, mayhap),
    cunningly structural – weakly helpful?]

Husband ye not one plant of the bushy tribe
First-before (or in) preference to the vine!
  [Sanity is a feeble weapon
    set against lunacy, nobly helpless.]